Title:
LinkedIn Sales Navigator Mastery:
The Ultimate Guide to Social Selling, Ideal Customer Profiling and LinkedIn Business Strategies

By Clinton A. Quentin

INTRODUCTION

Superheroes owe much of their effectiveness to their array of tools. Imagine Iron Man without his suit; he'd be just another CEO, referred to simply as "Mr. Stark." Similarly, LinkedIn Sales Navigator serves as a crucial tool when it comes to social selling, marketing, offering immense potential for enhancing sales strategies. However, mastering its intricacies requires effort, given its complexity.

LinkedIn Sales Navigator often remains untapped as a resource for prospecting, lead generation, and cultivating business connections. In my view, few tools on the market offer the same level of functionality and value for the price as Sales Navigator.

However, many individuals fail to harness Sales Navigator's full potential due to a lack of understanding of its capabilities.

When considering the inherent advantages of Sales Navigator, two aspects come to mind: targeting and messaging.

Imagine, if you will, a tool so potent that it transforms the mundane into the miraculous, the daunting into the doable. This is the promise of LinkedIn Sales Navigator – a promise of empowerment, of clarity amidst chaos, of triumph amidst uncertainty.

But what exactly is this enigmatic force that has captured the imagination of sales gurus and novices alike? It is more than just a platform; it is a conduit for connection, a gateway to opportunity, a compass navigating the tumultuous seas of modern sales.

Sales Navigator stands as LinkedIn's primary solution tailored for sales teams, offering representatives, managers, and operations leaders an array of tools to enhance their approaches and strategies. Through harnessing LinkedIn's extensive data, insights, and relationship-building capabilities, Sales Navigator empowers users to refine their sales tactics effectively.

For those seeking a comprehensive understanding of Sales Navigator's features, functionalities, and its role in facilitating Buyer First Selling, you've landed in the ideal spot. Whether you aim to grasp its offerings, delve into its workings, optimize its potential, or explore its role in prioritizing buyer-centric sales approaches, we're here to guide you every step of the way.

This guide unveils the discovery and transformation to unlocking the secrets of Sales Navigator and harnessing its full potential for success. From the humble beginnings of its conception to its meteoric rise as a cornerstone of modern sales strategy, we delve deep into the heart of this remarkable tool, peeling back the layers to reveal its inner workings and hidden treasures.

But this book is more than just a technical manual; it is a manifesto for change, a call to arms for sales professionals everywhere to embrace the power of Sales Navigator and embark on a journey of self-discovery and growth. For within these pages lie the keys to unlocking untold riches and unbridled success – if only you have the courage to seize them.

So, dear reader, I invite you to join me to explore and discover the secretes of modern sales together. For within the hallowed halls of LinkedIn Sales Navigator lie the answers to your deepest desires and wildest dreams – if only you have the wisdom to seek them out. Certainly being on this page together with me is a testament that you are on track.

Welcome aboard.

CHAPTER ONE

UNDERSTANDING LINKEDIN SALES NAVIGATOR

What Is Linkedin Sales Navigator?

LinkedIn Sales Navigator serves as a comprehensive sales platform, facilitating virtual selling by empowering sales professionals to cultivate and manage relationships with their buyers on a large scale. Positioned as a cornerstone for contemporary B2B sales teams, Sales Navigator seamlessly integrates with various sales technologies, including Customer Relationship Management (CRM) systems, to furnish users with a robust foundation of accurate, up-to-date data.

Considered the ultimate iteration of LinkedIn for sales professionals, Sales Navigator boasts a suite of robust search functionalities, enhanced visibility into extended networks, and personalized algorithms tailored to assist users in connecting with the appropriate decision-makers precisely when needed.

Sales Navigator is designed to empower sales professionals

in executing three vital functions essential to their role effectively.

- Firstly, it aids in targeting prospective clients swiftly by enabling users to identify and familiarize themselves with individuals and companies that align with their product or service offerings.
- Secondly, Sales Navigator facilitates understanding by enabling users to monitor key developments within target accounts. This includes tracking changes in decision-makers' roles and identifying signals indicating buying intent, allowing sales professionals to capitalize on emerging opportunities promptly.
- Lastly, the platform facilitates engagement by providing a conducive environment for connecting and interacting with prospects. Leveraging LinkedIn's messaging and content-sharing capabilities, users can engage with potential clients in a manner that fosters readiness to do business.

In an era where prioritizing the buyer's needs is paramount and virtual interactions have become commonplace, Sales Navigator serves as a valuable tool for salespeople. It equips them with the insights needed to lead effectively, deliver differentiated value, and cultivate relationships that drive customer acquisition.

Features of LinkedIn Sales Navigator

Sales Navigator offers a plethora of features designed

to enhance the day-to-day operations of you and your team. It is a powerhouse tool designed to empower sales professionals with a suite of features and tools tailored to their needs that make Sales Navigator an indispensable asset in the modern sales. These features are:

- **Extended Network Access:** Sales Navigator grants users access to LinkedIn's expansive global network of professionals. With unlimited searches, which can be saved for ongoing efficiency, users can tap into a vast pool of potential leads and connections.
- **Advanced Searching Tools:** Customize your search settings to suit your specific criteria and preferences. Utilizing advanced search filters and Sales Preferences, users can narrow down their searches based on parameters such as region, industry, function, and seniority level. This enables the platform to automatically surface relevant account and lead recommendations tailored to your preferences.
- **Prioritize and Qualify Opportunities:** Sales Navigator automatically highlights noteworthy results through Sales Spotlights. These highlights identify individuals who have recently changed jobs, share common experiences with you (such as alma mater or past employer), or have posted new content recently, helping users prioritize and qualify opportunities more effectively.
- **Outreach and Messaging:** While LinkedIn's native messaging tool, InMail, is available to all users, Sales Navigator enhances the opportunities to utilize InMail for initiating quick, personalized

conversations with new prospects. This feature facilitates seamless communication and engagement with potential leads.
- **Keep Track of People and Companies:** Users can save their most promising accounts and leads to receive real-time updates and alerts. Additionally, Sales Navigator allows users to create Custom Lists and record notes, enabling easy collaboration and information sharing across the team.
- **Lead Recommendations:** One of the standout features of Sales Navigator is its ability to provide personalized lead recommendations based on a user's saved searches, preferences, and past interactions. This feature helps users discover new prospects that align with their target criteria, saving time and effort in the prospecting process.
- **Real-time Insights and Alerts:** Sales Navigator keeps users informed with real-time updates on lead activity, job changes, and company news. These insights enable users to stay ahead of the curve and engage with prospects at the opportune moment, fostering more meaningful and timely interactions.
- **InMail Messaging:** Sales Navigator allows users to send direct messages, known as InMail, to prospects even if they're not connected on LinkedIn. This feature provides users with a valuable avenue for initiating conversations and building relationships with potential leads, bypassing traditional barriers to communication.
- **CRM Integration:** Sales Navigator seamlessly

integrates with popular Customer Relationship Management (CRM) platforms such as Salesforce, Microsoft Dynamics 365, and HubSpot. This integration enables users to sync their Sales Navigator data with their CRM systems, streamlining the lead management process and ensuring a seamless workflow.
- **Team Collaboration Features:** Sales Navigator offers features for team collaboration, allowing users to share leads, insights, and notes with their colleagues within the platform. This collaboration functionality promotes alignment and coordination among team members, enhancing overall productivity and effectiveness in sales efforts.

By leveraging these key features of Sales Navigator, sales professionals can streamline their processes, identify valuable opportunities, and engage with prospects more effectively, ultimately driving success in their sales endeavors.

Comparison With Linkedin Premium And Free Accounts

LinkedIn offers users three tiers of membership: Free, Premium, and Sales Navigator. Each tier provides varying levels of access to features and tools, catering to different needs and objectives.

1. **LinkedIn Free Account:** A LinkedIn Free Account provides basic access to the platform's networking and

job search capabilities. Users can create a profile, connect with other users, join groups, and access limited search functionalities. However, Free Accounts have limitations in terms of search filters, messaging capabilities, and access to premium features.

2. LinkedIn Premium Account: LinkedIn Premium offers enhanced features and tools beyond what is available in a Free Account. Premium members have access to additional search filters, such as expanded options for job titles and company size. They also receive more profile views per month, access to LinkedIn Learning courses, and the ability to see who's viewed their profile. However, Premium Accounts still have limitations compared to Sales Navigator, particularly in terms of advanced search capabilities and CRM integration.

3. LinkedIn Sales Navigator: Sales Navigator is LinkedIn's premium sales tool, specifically designed to help sales professionals identify, engage, and nurture leads more effectively. Unlike Free and Premium Accounts, Sales Navigator offers advanced search functionalities, lead recommendations, real-time insights, InMail messaging, CRM integration, and team collaboration features. These capabilities enable users to target and connect with prospects with greater precision and efficiency, ultimately driving sales and revenue growth.

Evolution And Development Of Sales

Navigator

LinkedIn Sales Navigator didn't emerge fully formed but rather evolved over time in response to the changing needs of sales professionals and the evolving landscape of digital sales.

In its nascent stages, Sales Navigator began as a humble feature within the broader LinkedIn platform, offering enhanced search capabilities and insights tailored specifically for sales professionals. This initial iteration laid the foundation for what would eventually become a cornerstone of modern sales strategy.

As the demand for more sophisticated sales tools grew, LinkedIn recognized the opportunity to expand and refine Sales Navigator into a standalone product. With each iteration, new features and functionalities were added, each designed to streamline the sales process and empower users to achieve greater success in their sales efforts.

Key milestones in the evolution of Sales Navigator include the introduction of advanced search filters, which allowed users to refine their searches based on criteria such as industry, company size, and job title. This marked a significant leap forward in the tool's capabilities, enabling users to identify and target their ideal prospects with unprecedented precision.

Another pivotal moment in the development of Sales Navigator was the integration of real-time insights and alerts. This feature provided users with timely updates on lead activity, job changes, and company news, empowering them to engage with prospects at the right moment and with the right message.

Over time, Sales Navigator continued to evolve, incorporating feedback from users and leveraging advances in technology to enhance its capabilities. Today, Sales Navigator stands as a testament to the power of innovation and adaptation, a testament to LinkedIn's commitment to empowering sales professionals with the tools they need to succeed in an increasingly competitive marketplace.

CHAPTER TWO

SETTING UP YOUR SALES NAVIGATOR ACCOUNT

Creating An Account

Creating an account on LinkedIn Sales Navigator is a straightforward process that begins with visiting the LinkedIn website and selecting the Sales Navigator option from the navigation menu. From there, users are prompted to sign in with their existing LinkedIn credentials or create a new account if they don't already have one.

Once signed in, users are guided through a series of steps to set up their Sales Navigator account. This includes providing basic information such as their name, email address, and company affiliation. Users may also be asked to verify their identity through a verification email or phone number.

After providing the necessary information, users are prompted to choose a subscription plan for Sales Navigator. LinkedIn offers several subscription options with varying features and pricing tiers, allowing users to select the plan that best suits their needs and budget.

Once a subscription plan is selected and payment information is provided, users are given access to their Sales Navigator dashboard, where they can begin exploring the various features and tools available to them. This includes advanced search functionality, lead recommendations, real-time insights, and more.

Optimizing Profile For Sales Success

Optimizing your profile for sales success on LinkedIn Sales Navigator is crucial for making a lasting impression on potential leads and prospects. Here are some key steps to ensure your profile stands out and effectively communicates your value proposition:

1. Professional Profile Photo: Choose a high-quality, professional-looking photo that reflects your personal brand and instills confidence in potential connections. A clear, friendly headshot with a neutral background is ideal for making a positive first impression.

2. Compelling Headline: Craft a concise and compelling headline that clearly communicates your role, expertise, and value proposition. Use keywords relevant to your industry and target audience to optimize your profile for searchability.

3. Detailed Summary: Write a compelling summary

that showcases your unique skills, experiences, and achievements. Highlight your expertise, passion for your work, and commitment to providing value to your clients or customers. Use storytelling techniques to engage readers and make your profile memorable.

4. Experience and Accomplishments: Provide detailed descriptions of your work experience, highlighting key accomplishments, responsibilities, and achievements. Use action verbs and quantifiable metrics to demonstrate your impact and effectiveness in previous roles.

5. Skills and Endorsements: List relevant skills and expertise that showcase your strengths and competencies. Encourage colleagues, clients, and connections to endorse your skills to enhance your credibility and authority in your field.

6. Optimized Keywords: Incorporate relevant keywords and phrases throughout your profile to improve its visibility in search results. Use keywords related to your industry, role, and target audience to ensure your profile appears in relevant searches.

7. Engaging Multimedia Content: Enhance your profile with engaging multimedia content, such as videos, presentations, and articles, to showcase your expertise and demonstrate thought leadership in your field.

Setting Preferences And Notifications

Setting preferences and notifications on LinkedIn Sales Navigator is essential for customizing your experience and staying informed about important updates and activities within your network. Here are some key aspects to consider when setting your preferences:

1. **Profile Visibility:** Decide how you want your profile to be visible to others on Sales Navigator. You can choose to make your profile visible to everyone, only to your network, or to specific connections.

2. **Email Notifications**: Customize your email notification settings to receive updates about profile views, messages, connection requests, and other relevant activities. You can choose the frequency and type of notifications you receive to suit your preferences and workflow.

3. **Lead Alerts:** Set up lead alerts to receive notifications when new leads match your saved searches or criteria. This allows you to stay proactive and reach out to potential prospects in a timely manner.

4. **Job Change Alerts:** Enable job change alerts to receive notifications when your saved leads change positions or companies. This helps you stay informed about changes within your target accounts and identify new opportunities for engagement.

5. **Company News Alerts:** Stay updated on company news and updates by setting up alerts for your saved

accounts. This allows you to monitor developments within your target companies and tailor your outreach efforts accordingly.

6. Customized Preferences: Take advantage of Sales Navigator's customizable preferences to tailor your experience to your specific needs and preferences. You can adjust settings related to search filters, account preferences, and communication preferences to optimize your workflow and efficiency.

By carefully setting your preferences and notifications on LinkedIn Sales Navigator, you can ensure that you stay informed and engaged with relevant activities within your network. This allows you to maintain a proactive approach to sales and relationship-building, ultimately driving success and growth in your business endeavors.

Syncing With Crm Systems

Syncing LinkedIn Sales Navigator with CRM systems is a strategic move that can significantly enhance the efficiency and effectiveness of your sales efforts. Here's how the process works:

1. Integration Setup: The first step in syncing Sales Navigator with your CRM system is to set up the integration. Most CRM platforms offer integration options for Sales Navigator, allowing you to connect the two systems seamlessly.

2. Data Synchronization: Once the integration is set up, Sales Navigator and your CRM system will begin to sync data automatically. This includes information such as lead profiles, interactions, notes, and activities.

3. Lead Management: By syncing Sales Navigator with your CRM system, you can manage leads more effectively and efficiently. New leads identified on Sales Navigator can be automatically imported into your CRM system, allowing you to track and manage them alongside your existing leads and contacts.

4. Activity Tracking: Sales Navigator activities, such as profile views, messages, and InMail communications, are synced with your CRM system, providing a comprehensive view of your interactions with leads and prospects. This allows you to track engagement metrics and follow up with leads in a timely manner.

5. Lead Nurturing: With Sales Navigator and CRM integration, you can create targeted lead nurturing campaigns based on insights and data from both systems. This allows you to personalize your outreach efforts and engage leads more effectively throughout the sales cycle.

6. Pipeline Management: Integration with CRM systems enables you to track leads through the sales pipeline more effectively. You can monitor lead progression, update lead statuses, and track sales opportunities within your CRM system, providing greater visibility and control over your

sales process.

7. Reporting and Analytics: Integrated Sales Navigator and CRM systems provide robust reporting and analytics capabilities, allowing you to analyze sales performance, track ROI, and identify areas for improvement. This data-driven approach enables you to make informed decisions and optimize your sales strategies for maximum impact.

In summary, syncing LinkedIn Sales Navigator with CRM systems is a strategic move that can streamline lead management, improve lead nurturing efforts, and enhance overall sales effectiveness. By integrating Sales Navigator with your CRM system, you can leverage the combined power of these tools to drive success and achieve your sales goals.

CHAPTER THREE

LEVERAGING ADVANCED SEARCH TECHNIQUES

Understanding Search Filters And Parameters

Search filters and parameters on LinkedIn Sales Navigator are the essential tools that enable users to refine their searches and uncover valuable prospects with precision.

How To Use Advanced Search Filters

1. Industry: The industry filter allows users to narrow down their search results based on specific industries or sectors. This helps users focus their efforts on prospects within their target industries, allowing for more relevant and targeted outreach.

Initially, when I began utilizing LinkedIn Sales Navigator, I heavily relied on the Industry filter. However, as many users may have encountered, there are certain quirks associated with this filter that render it less dependable.

While the Industry filter serves as a broad filter when

accurate, its reliability is not absolute. A significant drawback of this filter is its reliance on self-reported data, which introduces potential inaccuracies.

In many cases, a more precise targeting approach can be achieved by utilizing Boolean Search within the Company filter. Nonetheless, I still resort to the Industry filter when I need to refine a lengthy list or when the terms I've applied in the Company filter span multiple industries. In such instances, the Industry filter aids in ensuring I target a specific niche effectively.

For example, if my aim is to target distribution companies within the Food & Beverages sector, I would input "Distribution" into the Company filter and "Food & Beverages" into the Industry filter. While the Industry filter serves as a useful supplementary tool, it's important to acknowledge its limitations and avoid relying solely on it for precise targeting.

2. Company Size:

The company size filter enables users to filter search results based on the size of the companies they are interested in targeting. Users can specify company size based on various parameters, such as the number of employees or annual revenue, to tailor their search to their specific preferences and objectives.

The Company filter may initially seem perplexing to some

users, yet it has proven to yield superior results compared to the Industry filter in my experience. This can be attributed to various factors, including individuals holding multiple concurrent positions across different industries.

Hence, I advocate for acquainting oneself with the Company filter and experimenting with its functionalities firsthand. It's worth noting that the Company filter supports Boolean Search, offering a wealth of possibilities for customization.

An illustrative example where I've observed the Company filter outperforming the Industry filter is when targeting Hospitals. Instead of relying solely on the Industry filter, I prefer to input specific terms such as Hospital, Medical Center, and Clinic into the Company filter. This approach ensures precise targeting, as I can directly identify the relevant companies within my search results.

Consider another scenario where you aim to target tech companies featuring domain extensions like ".io" or ".ai" in their LinkedIn company names. The potential applications of this approach are boundless, allowing for creative strategies to attain precise search outcomes. However, it's essential to note that while utilizing both the Company filter and the Industry filter concurrently may seem beneficial, it could inadvertently restrict your search results.

Here are a few additional examples to illustrate the versatility of the Company filter:

- When targeting manufacturing companies, consider inputting "Manufacturing" into the Company filter to streamline your search results.
- If your focus is on identifying lawyers operating within small practices, incorporating "Lawyer" into the Title filter and "Associates" into the Company filter can refine your search parameters effectively.

The versatility and expansive potential of the Company filter render it an invaluable tool, yet it remains vastly underutilized.

3. Job Title: The job title filter allows users to target prospects based on their job titles or positions within an organization. Users can specify specific titles or job roles relevant to their target audience, enabling them to connect with decision-makers and key stakeholders more effectively.

The Title filter holds a special place in my toolkit—it's what I consider my "golden" filter. If I were to select just one filter from Sales Navigator, this would undoubtedly be my top choice.

The versatility of the Title filter is truly remarkable, allowing for a wide range of applications. Let me illustrate with a few examples. What makes the Title filter particularly potent is its compatibility with Boolean Search.

For instance, if I'm seeking Transplant Directors but wish to exclude individuals associated with Hair Transplant, I can employ a search query to specifically target directors while filtering out irrelevant roles. Here's another scenario: Suppose I aim to target Chief Marketing Officers while excluding those also involved in Sales or Business Development. By refining my search to focus solely on marketing professionals, I can ensure that my results align with my criteria.

Here's a community insider tip: As you fine-tune your Title searches to meet your precise requirements, it's beneficial to scroll through multiple pages of search results. Pay close attention to the titles of your prospects, and if you notice any discrepancies, take proactive steps to exclude them from your search parameters. For instance, I often exclude terms like "coaches" or "consultants" to maintain the cleanliness and relevance of my search results.

4. Location:

The location filter enables users to narrow down their search results based on geographic location. Users can specify regions, countries, cities, or even specific postal codes to focus their search on prospects within their desired location.

Among the fundamental filters available, Geography stands out as a cornerstone in constructing a targeted search. While seemingly basic, it's noteworthy due to its pivotal role in refining searches. An often overlooked feature within this category is the option to filter by specific Postal Codes.

The utility of Postal Code filtering is particularly advantageous for brick-and-mortar businesses tethered to physical locations or sales professionals operating within specific regions. For instance, envision a scenario where a Real Estate Agent leverages the Postal Code filter to connect with the most active LinkedIn members within their local community.

5. Keywords: Keywords are another important search parameter that users can utilize to refine their search queries. Users can include specific keywords or phrases related to their industry, products, or services to identify prospects who are likely to be interested in what they have to offer.

6. Connections: The connections filter allows users to filter search results based on their existing connections on LinkedIn. Users can choose to include or exclude connections from their search results, helping them focus

on reaching out to new prospects rather than contacting individuals they already know.

Crafting Effective Search Queries

Crafting effective search queries on LinkedIn Sales Navigator is crucial for uncovering valuable prospects and maximizing the impact of your outreach efforts. Here are some key strategies to help you craft search queries that yield meaningful results:

1. Define Your Objective: Start by clarifying your objective and identifying the specific criteria you're looking for in potential leads. Whether you're targeting a particular industry, company size, job title, or geographic location, having a clear objective will help you narrow down your search parameters and refine your query accordingly.

2. Use Relevant Keywords: Incorporate relevant keywords and phrases into your search query to target prospects who are likely to be interested in your products or services. Consider the language and terminology commonly used in your industry or niche, and include keywords that align with your target audience's interests and needs.

3. Utilize Boolean Operators: Boolean operators, such as AND, OR, and NOT, can be used to refine your search query and include or exclude specific terms or criteria. For example, using "AND" between two search terms will return results that include both terms, while using "NOT"

before a term will exclude results containing that term.

4. Combine Filters for Precision: Combine multiple search filters to create highly targeted queries that align with your ideal customer profile. For example, you can filter your search results based on industry, company size, and job title to narrow down your prospects to those who meet all of your criteria.

5. Experiment and Iterate: Don't be afraid to experiment with different combinations of filters and keywords to see which ones yield the best results. Sales Navigator allows you to save your search queries and revisit them later, so you can iterate and refine your searches over time based on feedback and results.

6. Review and Refine Results: Once you've run your search query, take the time to review and refine your results to ensure they align with your objectives and criteria. Look for patterns or trends in the data, and adjust your search parameters as needed to improve the relevance and accuracy of your results.

Targeting Specific Industries, Companies, And Roles

Targeting specific industries, companies, and roles on LinkedIn Sales Navigator is a strategic approach that allows sales professionals to focus their efforts on reaching prospects who are most likely to be interested in their products or services.

1. Identify Relevant Industries: Start by identifying the industries that are most relevant to your target market. Consider factors such as industry trends, market demand, and your own expertise and experience. By focusing on industries that align with your offerings and expertise, you can maximize the impact of your outreach efforts and increase the likelihood of success.

2. Research Target Companies: Once you've identified relevant industries, research specific companies within those industries that are a good fit for your products or services. Look for companies that have a need or pain point that your offerings can address, and prioritize those companies in your outreach efforts.

3. Define Target Roles: Next, define the specific roles within your target companies that are most likely to be involved in the decision-making process for purchasing your products or services. This may include roles such as CEOs, CMOs, CFOs, or other key decision-makers. By targeting individuals in these roles, you can ensure that your message reaches the right audience and resonates with their needs and priorities.

4. Utilize Advanced Search Filters: Sales Navigator offers advanced search filters that allow you to narrow down your search results based on specific industries, companies, and roles. Take advantage of these filters to create highly

targeted searches that focus on your ideal prospects. You can also use additional filters such as company size, location, and keywords to further refine your search criteria and ensure that you're targeting the right audience.

5. Personalize Your Outreach: Once you've identified your target industries, companies, and roles, personalize your outreach messages to resonate with your prospects' needs and interests. Tailor your messaging to address specific pain points or challenges that your prospects may be facing, and highlight how your products or services can provide value and solve their problems.

By targeting specific industries, companies, and roles on LinkedIn Sales Navigator, you can focus your efforts on reaching prospects who are most likely to be interested in what you have to offer. By leveraging advanced search filters and personalizing your outreach messages, you can increase the effectiveness of your sales efforts and achieve greater success in driving engagement and conversions.

Using Boolean Operators For Advanced Searches

Boolean operators are powerful tools that allow users to refine their search queries and uncover more targeted results on LinkedIn Sales Navigator. Here's how you can effectively use Boolean operators to conduct advanced searches:

1. AND Operator: The AND operator is used to narrow down search results by requiring that both terms or criteria are present in the search results. For example, if you're searching for prospects who are both in the "technology" industry and hold the title of "CEO," you can use the AND operator to find individuals who meet both criteria. Your search query would look like this: "technology AND CEO."

2. OR Operator: The OR operator is used to broaden search results by including either of the terms or criteria in the search results. For example, if you're searching for prospects who are either in the "technology" or "finance" industries, you can use the OR operator to find individuals who meet either criteria. Your search query would look like this: "technology OR finance."

3. NOT Operator: The NOT operator is used to exclude specific terms or criteria from the search results. For example, if you're searching for prospects in the "technology" industry but want to exclude individuals with the title of "intern," you can use the NOT operator to exclude that term from your search results. Your search query would look like this: "technology NOT intern."

4. Parentheses for Grouping: Parentheses can be used to group terms or criteria together and specify the order of operations in complex search queries. For example, if you're searching for prospects who are either in the "technology" industry and hold the title of "CEO," or are in

the "finance" industry and hold the title of "CFO," you can use parentheses to group the terms together and specify the OR operator between them. Your search query would look like this: "(technology AND CEO) OR (finance AND CFO)."

By using Boolean operators effectively in your search queries on LinkedIn Sales Navigator, you can conduct more targeted and precise searches to uncover valuable prospects that meet your specific criteria. Whether you're narrowing down your search results with the AND operator, broadening your search with the OR operator, or excluding specific terms with the NOT operator, leveraging Boolean operators allows you to tailor your searches to your unique needs and objectives, ultimately driving greater success in your sales efforts.

CHAPTER FOUR

GENERATING LEADS AND PROSPECTS

Identifying Ideal Customer Profiles (Icps)

In the realm of B2B marketing, account-based marketing (ABM) revolves around the concept of an Ideal Customer Profile (ICP), which outlines the characteristics of a company deemed a perfect match for the products or services offered. This profile is sometimes referred to as an Ideal Buyer Profile, but the underlying principle remains consistent: identifying the most suitable customer for your business.

Typically, an ICP represents an imaginary company that embodies the epitome of an ideal lead—the type of lead most likely to be receptive to your sales efforts, possessing the ideal combination of budget, scale, location, and requirements.

Various factors contribute to defining your Ideal Customer Profile, including considerations such as legal conflicts of interest (for instance, if you currently serve one company that would object to you working with a competitor), geographic limitations, and your ability to accommodate their scheduling constraints.

Building An Ideal Customer Profile

Developing an Ideal Customer Profile (ICP) is a crucial step in targeting the right audience effectively. While it may seem like a daunting task, it can be simplified by leveraging existing operational data and engaging key stakeholders from various teams, including customer success, sales, and marketing.

Here's how to get started:

Identify Your Core Competencies:

Begin by assessing your organization's core competencies and the solutions it offers. What problems does your organization solve? Understanding your strengths will help pinpoint your target audience and how your offerings can address their needs. Be specific in this analysis. For instance, if you offer accountancy software, consider whether it caters best to multinational corporations with extensive employee bases or to independent startups.

Analyze Your Best Customers:

One of the most effective methods for defining your Ideal Customer Profile is to examine your top-performing existing customers. Identify your most successful accounts—those with the highest customer lifetime value or those who consistently return for your services. Look for common characteristics among these customers, including:

- Geographic location and any associated restrictions
- Industry
- Company size (number of employees and customer base)
- Revenue and budget
- Existing technology stack
- These shared characteristics among your best customers serve as the foundation for your Ideal Customer Profile.

By following these steps and involving key stakeholders in the process, you can create a robust Ideal Customer Profile that aligns with your organization's strengths and targets the most promising prospects effectively.

What Insights Does Your Customer Feedback Provide?

Finally, delve into metrics such as Net Promoter Score (NPS), Customer Satisfaction (CSAT), and qualitative customer feedback to validate your assessments. Essentially, you want to ensure that the customers you perceive as your most successful accounts share the same sentiment.

Ideally, this customer feedback aligns with your operational and sales data, providing robust historical examples of customers that closely resemble your ideal profile. These examples serve as a solid foundation for crafting your written Ideal Customer Profile (ICP).

Identifying Ideal Customer Profiles (ICPs) is a crucial step in any sales strategy, as it helps businesses target their efforts towards the most promising prospects.

1. Define Your Ideal Customer: Start by defining your ideal customer based on factors such as industry, company size, job title, geographic location, and any other relevant criteria. Consider the characteristics of your most successful customers, as well as the needs and pain points that your products or services address.

2. Conduct Market Research: Conduct thorough market research to gather insights into your target market and industry landscape. Identify trends, patterns, and opportunities within your target market, and use this information to refine your understanding of your ideal customer profile.

3. Analyze Existing Customer Data: Analyze your existing customer data to identify common traits, behaviors, and characteristics among your most successful customers. Look for patterns and correlations in your data to uncover

key insights into what makes a customer an ideal fit for your business.

4. Create Buyer Personas: Develop buyer personas that represent different segments of your target audience based on their demographics, needs, preferences, and behaviors. Use these personas to create a clear picture of who your ideal customers are and what motivates them to engage with your business.

5. Refine and Iterate: Continuously refine and iterate your ideal customer profile based on feedback, insights, and changes in the market landscape. Stay flexible and open to adjusting your criteria as you learn more about your target audience and their evolving needs and preferences.

6. Align Sales and Marketing Efforts: Ensure alignment between your sales and marketing efforts by sharing insights and collaborating on the development of ICPs. Use ICPs to guide your lead generation, prospecting, and outreach efforts, and tailor your messaging and content to resonate with your ideal customers.

Utilizing Lead Recommendations

Utilizing lead recommendations on LinkedIn Sales Navigator is a powerful way to discover new prospects and expand your network of potential customers. Here's how you can effectively leverage lead recommendations to enhance your sales efforts:

1. **Accessing Lead Recommendations:** Lead recommendations are suggestions provided by Sales Navigator based on your saved searches, preferences, and past interactions. You can access lead recommendations directly from your Sales Navigator dashboard, where they are conveniently displayed for easy access.

2. **Reviewing Recommendations:** Take the time to review the lead recommendations provided by Sales Navigator carefully. Pay attention to factors such as relevance, fit with your ideal customer profile, and potential for engagement. Prioritize leads that align closely with your target criteria and are likely to be interested in your products or services.

3. **Exploring Insights and Data:** Dive deeper into each lead recommendation to explore additional insights and data provided by Sales Navigator. This may include information such as mutual connections, recent activity, and shared interests or affiliations. Use this information to personalize your outreach efforts and tailor your messaging to resonate with each prospect's unique needs and interests.

4. **Engaging with Prospects:** Once you've identified promising leads from the recommendations provided by Sales Navigator, take proactive steps to engage with them. Send personalized connection requests or InMail messages to introduce yourself, establish rapport, and initiate conversations. Be genuine, authentic, and value-driven in your communications to build trust and credibility with your prospects.

5. Tracking and Monitoring Results: Keep track of your interactions with leads recommended by Sales Navigator and monitor the outcomes of your outreach efforts. Track metrics such as response rates, engagement levels, and conversion rates to assess the effectiveness of your sales tactics and refine your approach over time.

6. Iterating and Refining Strategies: Continuously iterate and refine your lead generation strategies based on feedback, insights, and results. Adjust your targeting criteria, messaging strategies, and outreach tactics as needed to optimize your efforts and maximize your success in converting leads into customers.

Engaging With Warm Leads And Connections

Engaging with warm leads and connections on LinkedIn Sales Navigator is an essential step in building relationships, fostering trust, and ultimately driving conversions.

1. Personalized Outreach: When reaching out to warm leads and connections, personalize your messages to demonstrate genuine interest and establish rapport. Reference shared connections, mutual interests, or recent activities to create a connection and make your outreach more relevant and meaningful.

2. Provide Value: Focus on providing value to your warm leads and connections by offering insights, resources, or

solutions that address their needs and challenges. Share relevant content, offer helpful advice, or provide access to exclusive resources to demonstrate your expertise and build trust.

3. Ask Open-Ended Questions: Encourage engagement and conversation by asking open-ended questions that prompt your warm leads and connections to share their thoughts, opinions, and experiences. Listen actively to their responses and use the insights gained to tailor your approach and deepen the relationship.

4. Offer Assistance: Be proactive in offering assistance and support to your warm leads and connections. Offer to provide guidance, answer questions, or connect them with relevant resources or contacts that can help them achieve their goals. By demonstrating your willingness to help, you can strengthen your relationship and position yourself as a trusted advisor.

5. Follow Up Consistently: Stay top-of-mind with your warm leads and connections by following up consistently and staying engaged over time. Send follow-up messages, share relevant updates, and continue to provide value to maintain momentum and nurture the relationship.

6. Monitor Engagement Metrics: Keep track of engagement metrics such as response rates, message open rates, and interaction levels to assess the effectiveness of your outreach efforts. Use this data to refine your approach,

optimize your messaging, and tailor your strategies to better resonate with your audience.

7. Build Relationships: Focus on building genuine, authentic relationships with your warm leads and connections rather than focusing solely on sales objectives. Invest time in getting to know them, understanding their needs and preferences, and finding ways to add value to their lives and businesses.

Strategies For Cold Outreach And Inmail Messaging

Cold outreach and InMail messaging are essential components of any sales strategy, allowing you to connect with prospects who may not be familiar with your brand or offerings.

1. Personalization: Personalize your outreach messages to demonstrate that you've done your research and understand the recipient's needs and interests. Mention specific details from their profile or recent activities to make your message more relevant and engaging.

2. Value Proposition: Clearly communicate the value proposition of your product or service in your outreach messages. Highlight the benefits and solutions that you can provide to address the recipient's pain points or challenges, and explain how your offering can help them achieve their goals.

3. **Clear Call-to-Action (CTA)**: Include a clear and compelling call-to-action (CTA) in your outreach messages to prompt the recipient to take the desired next step. Whether it's scheduling a call, requesting more information, or signing up for a demo, make it easy for the recipient to respond and engage with you.

4. **Concise and Compelling Messaging**: Keep your outreach messages concise and to the point, focusing on the most important information and avoiding unnecessary jargon or filler. Use compelling language and storytelling techniques to capture the recipient's attention and encourage them to take action.

5. **Follow-Up**: Don't be discouraged if you don't receive a response to your initial outreach message. Follow up with the recipient after a few days to remind them of your offer and reiterate the value proposition. Persistence pays off in cold outreach, so don't be afraid to follow up multiple times if necessary.

6. **Test and Iterate**: Experiment with different messaging strategies, subject lines, and CTAs to see what resonates best with your target audience. Test different approaches and track the results to identify what works and what doesn't, and iterate on your messaging accordingly.

7. **Timing and Frequency**: Pay attention to the timing and frequency of your outreach messages to maximize your chances of success. Avoid sending messages during

busy times or holidays when recipients are likely to be overwhelmed with other priorities. Instead, aim to send messages at times when recipients are more likely to be receptive, such as during regular business hours.

By implementing these strategies for cold outreach and InMail messaging on LinkedIn Sales Navigator, you can increase your chances of engaging with prospects, generating leads, and ultimately driving sales. With a combination of personalization, value proposition, clear CTAs, and persistence, you can effectively leverage cold outreach to expand your network and grow your business.

CHAPTER FIVE

HARNESSING REAL-TIME INSIGHTS FOR ACTIONABLE INTELLIGENCE

Monitoring Lead Activity And Engagement

Monitoring lead activity and engagement is a critical aspect of any sales strategy, as it allows you to track the behavior and interactions of your leads and prospects.

1. Use Sales Navigator Tools: LinkedIn Sales Navigator offers a range of tools and features that allow you to track lead activity and engagement. Take advantage of features such as the "Lead Recommendations" tab, which provides insights into new prospects who match your ideal customer profile, and the "Notifications" tab, which alerts you to any new interactions or updates from your leads.

2. Set Up Saved Searches and Alerts: Set up saved searches and alerts based on specific criteria to stay informed about new leads and prospects who match your target profile. This allows you to proactively monitor for new opportunities and reach out to prospects in a timely

manner.

3. Monitor Profile Views and InMail Responses: Keep an eye on the number of profile views and responses to your InMail messages to gauge the level of interest and engagement from your leads. Track metrics such as open rates, response rates, and click-through rates to assess the effectiveness of your outreach efforts and identify areas for improvement.

4. Track Engagement on Content: Monitor engagement on the content you share on LinkedIn, such as likes, comments, and shares. Pay attention to the types of content that resonate most with your audience and generate the highest levels of engagement, and use this insight to inform your content strategy and future outreach efforts.

5. Use CRM Integration: If you use a Customer Relationship Management (CRM) system, integrate it with LinkedIn Sales Navigator to track lead activity and engagement in one centralized location. This allows you to easily view and manage your leads' interactions across multiple channels and streamline your sales process.

6. Follow Up Promptly: Actively monitor lead activity and engagement to identify opportunities for follow-up and engagement. When a lead takes a specific action, such as viewing your profile or responding to an InMail message, take prompt action to continue the conversation and move

the relationship forward.

7. Regularly Review and Analyze Data: Regularly review and analyze the data collected from your lead monitoring efforts to identify trends, patterns, and opportunities. Use this data to refine your targeting criteria, adjust your messaging strategies, and optimize your outreach tactics for maximum effectiveness.

Tracking Company News And Updates

Tracking company news and updates is a valuable strategy for staying informed about developments and changes within your target companies.

1. Follow Target Companies: Start by following the companies that are of interest to you or are relevant to your target market. When you follow a company on LinkedIn, you'll receive notifications about their updates, such as new hires, product launches, or company announcements, directly in your feed.

2. Set Up Company Alerts: Take advantage of the company alert feature on LinkedIn Sales Navigator to receive notifications whenever there are new updates from your followed companies. You can customize your alerts based on specific criteria, such as changes in company size, key personnel, or industry news, to ensure that you're notified about the most relevant updates.

3. Monitor Company Pages: Regularly monitor the company pages of your target companies to stay updated on their latest news and updates. Company pages often contain valuable information about the company's products, services, culture, and recent developments, providing valuable insights into their activities and priorities.

4. Engage with Company Content: Engage with the content shared by your target companies on LinkedIn by liking, commenting, or sharing their posts. This not only helps you stay informed about their updates but also helps you build relationships and establish credibility with key stakeholders within the company.

5. Use Search Filters: Use the search filters on LinkedIn Sales Navigator to discover relevant news and updates from your target companies. You can filter your search results based on specific criteria, such as industry, location, or company size, to narrow down your focus and find the most relevant information.

6. Track Competitor Activity: Keep an eye on the activity of your competitors as well, as their news and updates can provide valuable insights into market trends, customer preferences, and potential opportunities. Use LinkedIn Sales Navigator to track competitor activity and stay informed about their latest developments.

7. Stay Proactive and Engaged: Stay proactive in monitoring

company news and updates on LinkedIn Sales Navigator, and be proactive in engaging with your target companies. Use the insights gained from tracking company news to inform your sales and marketing strategies, identify opportunities for engagement, and stay ahead of the competition.

Leveraging Job Change Alerts For Opportunities

Leveraging job change alerts on LinkedIn Sales Navigator is a strategic approach to identifying potential opportunities and building relationships with professionals who are experiencing career transitions.

Receive Timely Notifications: LinkedIn Sales Navigator provides timely notifications when individuals in your network or target audience change jobs or roles. These notifications are valuable indicators of potential opportunities to engage with these individuals and explore new business prospects.

Identify Relevant Contacts: Pay attention to job change alerts from individuals who are relevant to your business objectives or target audience. Look for professionals who hold decision-making roles or have influence within their organizations, as they may represent valuable opportunities for partnership, collaboration, or sales.

Reach Out with Congratulations: When you receive a job

change alert, take the opportunity to reach out to the individual with a congratulatory message. Acknowledge their career milestone and express genuine interest in their new role or responsibilities. This initial contact sets the stage for further engagement and relationship-building.

Offer Value and Support: In your outreach message, offer value and support to the individual in their new role. Share relevant resources, insights, or connections that can help them succeed in their new position. By demonstrating your willingness to add value, you can begin to establish credibility and trust with the individual.

Explore Potential Opportunities: Use job change alerts as an opportunity to explore potential business opportunities with the individual. Depending on their new role or company, there may be opportunities for collaboration, partnership, or sales that align with your business objectives. Initiate a conversation to explore these possibilities further.

Stay Connected: Stay connected with individuals who have experienced a job change by continuing to engage with them on LinkedIn. Like, comment, and share their posts, and reach out periodically to check in and maintain the relationship. By staying top-of-mind, you can position yourself as a trusted resource and valuable connection for the individual.

Monitor Trends and Patterns: Monitor trends and patterns

in job changes within your target industry or market segment. Look for commonalities or trends that may indicate emerging opportunities or areas of growth. Use this insight to inform your sales and marketing strategies and stay ahead of the curve.

Using Insights to Personalize Outreach and Conversations

Using insights to personalize outreach and conversations is a powerful way to connect with prospects on a deeper level and drive more meaningful interactions.

1. Gather Relevant Information: Start by gathering relevant information about your prospects from LinkedIn Sales Navigator and other sources. Pay attention to details such as their job title, company, industry, location, interests, and recent activities. The more you know about your prospects, the better you can tailor your outreach and conversations to their specific needs and interests.

2. Segment Your Audience: Segment your audience based on common characteristics or interests to ensure that your outreach messages are relevant and targeted. For example, you may segment your audience based on industry, job title, or level of seniority. This allows you to craft personalized messages that resonate with each segment of your audience.

3. Tailor Your Messaging: Use the insights you've gathered to tailor your messaging to each individual prospect. Reference specific details from their profile or recent activities to demonstrate that you've done your research and understand their needs and interests. Personalize your message to address their pain points, challenges, or goals, and highlight how your product or service can provide value and solve their problems.

4. Provide Relevant Content: Share relevant content with your prospects that aligns with their interests or challenges. This could include articles, case studies, whitepapers, or blog posts that provide insights or solutions related to their industry or role. By providing valuable content, you demonstrate your expertise and establish credibility with your prospects.

5. Ask Thoughtful Questions: Engage your prospects in meaningful conversations by asking thoughtful questions that demonstrate your genuine interest in their needs and objectives. Use the insights you've gathered to ask relevant questions that prompt them to share more about their challenges, goals, and priorities. Listen actively to their responses and use the information gained to guide the conversation and tailor your offerings to their specific needs.

6. Follow Up with Relevance: Follow up with your prospects in a timely manner, and continue to personalize your outreach based on their responses and interactions.

Reference previous conversations or interactions to demonstrate continuity and build rapport. Provide additional insights or resources that address their needs or interests, and keep the conversation focused on how you can add value and help them achieve their goals.

7. Track and Analyze Results: Track the results of your personalized outreach efforts and analyze the impact on engagement, conversion, and overall sales performance. Pay attention to metrics such as response rates, meeting bookings, and conversion rates to assess the effectiveness of your personalized approach and identify areas for improvement. Use this data to refine your strategies and optimize your outreach efforts over time.

By leveraging insights to personalize your outreach and conversations on LinkedIn Sales Navigator, you can create deeper connections with your prospects, drive more meaningful interactions, and ultimately increase your chances of success in converting leads into customers. With a proactive approach to gathering and using insights, you can tailor your messaging and offerings to the specific needs and interests of your target audience, ultimately driving greater engagement and driving business growth.

CHAPTER SIX

INTEGRATING SALES NAVIGATOR WITH CRM SYSTEMS

Overview Of Crm Integration Options

Sales Navigator serves as a robust resource empowering sales professionals to discover leads and establish meaningful engagements with them. By integrating Sales Navigator with your Customer Relationship Management (CRM) system, you can elevate your sales process, facilitating seamless lead management, progress tracking, and accelerated deal closures. In this piece, we will delve into the process of integrating Sales Navigator with your CRM and delve into the myriad benefits associated with this integration.

Advantages Of Integrating Sales Navigator With Your Crm

Linking Sales Navigator with your CRM system offers a

plethora of advantages, including:

Enhanced Lead Management

Through the integration of Sales Navigator with your CRM, you gain the ability to monitor leads' journey from initiation to conversion comprehensively. This empowers you to track their progress, identify potential obstacles or bottlenecks, and refine your sales strategies accordingly.

Improved Data Accuracy

Integration ensures that all lead data remains current and precise within your CRM. This eradicates the need for manual data input, which is prone to errors and time-consuming.

Heightened Efficiency

The fusion of Sales Navigator with your CRM optimizes your sales processes, reducing the time and resources required for lead management. This, in turn, allows your sales team to allocate more time to their core competency: selling.

Facilitated Collaboration

Integration guarantees that all team members have access to the same dataset, fostering collaboration and coherence within your team. This unified approach enables your team to operate more seamlessly and efficiently.

Guidelines For Optimizing Sales Navigator Integration With Your Crm

To achieve seamless and efficient integration, adhere to the following guidelines:

1. Define Your Sales Workflow:
Before initiating the integration process, clearly outline your sales workflow. This entails identifying key data points crucial to your sales process and determining their method of tracking within your CRM.

2. Provide Adequate Training:
Ensure that your sales team receives comprehensive training on both Sales Navigator and your CRM platform. This equips them with the necessary skills to leverage the integration effectively, fostering uniformity and maximizing its potential.

3. Maintain Data Integrity:
Maintaining the integrity of your data is paramount for accurate reporting and forecasting. Regularly audit and update your data to eliminate inconsistencies and ensure its accuracy, thus enhancing the reliability of your insights and analytics.

How To Integrate Sales Navigator With Your Crm

Integrating Sales Navigator with your CRM is a straightforward process. Below is a step-by-step guide to help you get started:

Select Your CRM Platform

Sales Navigator offers integration with several popular CRM platforms, including Salesforce, Microsoft Dynamics, and HubSpot. Choose the CRM that aligns best with your business needs and sign up for an account if you haven't already done so.

Establish Connection Between Sales Navigator and Your CRM

After selecting your CRM, the next step is to establish a connection between Sales Navigator and your chosen CRM platform. Typically, this is achieved through an integration or plugin available within your CRM's interface.

Import Your Leads

Once the connection is established, you can commence the process of importing your leads. This involves selecting the leads you wish to import from Sales Navigator and mapping them to the corresponding fields within your CRM.

Ensure Data Synchronization

After importing your leads, it's crucial to verify that data synchronization is functioning correctly between Sales Navigator and your CRM. This ensures that any modifications or updates made in either system are promptly reflected in the other, maintaining data consistency across both platforms.

Below is a guide illustrating how to link Sales Navigator with Salesforce:

- Sign in to your Salesforce account and proceed to the AppExchange.
- Search for the Sales Navigator application and click on "Get It Now" to initiate the installation process.
- Upon successful installation, navigate to the Sales Navigator dashboard and access "Admin Settings."
- Locate and select "CRM Sync," then designate "Salesforce" as your CRM platform.
- Follow the on-screen instructions to input your Salesforce credentials and authorize the integration.
- Once the integration is authorized, you'll have the option to specify which Salesforce fields you wish to synchronize with Sales Navigator.
- Additionally, you can configure automated data synchronization between the two systems and determine the direction of data flow—either from Sales Navigator to Salesforce or vice versa.

Upon completion of the integration setup, you'll notice the seamless exchange of data between Sales Navigator and Salesforce. It's essential to recognize that the precise steps for connecting Sales Navigator with Salesforce may vary based on your subscription level and the Salesforce version you are utilizing. For optimal results, consider seeking guidance from a technical specialist or adhering to the instructions provided by Sales Navigator and Salesforce to ensure accurate integration setup.

Setting Up Integration With Salesforce, Microsoft Dynamics 365, Etc

Setting up integration with CRM systems like Salesforce and Microsoft Dynamics 365 is essential for streamlining sales and marketing processes and ensuring seamless data flow between LinkedIn Sales Navigator and your CRM platform.

Here's how you can set up integration with these CRM systems:

1. Choose the Integration Method: Determine the integration method that best suits your needs and requirements. Most CRM systems offer native integration options, as well as third-party integration tools and APIs for custom integration. Assess the available options and choose the method that aligns with your technical capabilities and business objectives.

2. Access Integration Settings: Access the integration settings within your CRM system to initiate the integration process. Depending on the CRM platform, you may find

integration settings in the admin or settings menu, where you can configure connections with external applications like LinkedIn Sales Navigator.

3. Authorize Access: To establish integration with LinkedIn Sales Navigator, you'll need to authorize access to your CRM system. Follow the prompts to log in to your LinkedIn Sales Navigator account and grant permission for the integration to access your CRM data. This step ensures secure and authenticated access to your CRM system.

4. Map Data Fields: Once access is authorized, you'll need to map data fields between LinkedIn Sales Navigator and your CRM system. This involves aligning fields such as contact information, company details, and activity logs to ensure accurate data synchronization between the two platforms. Review and configure field mappings to match your CRM data structure and preferences.

5. Set up Synchronization Rules: Define synchronization rules to govern the flow of data between LinkedIn Sales Navigator and your CRM system. Specify criteria for data syncing, such as frequency of updates, types of data to be synchronized, and filters for excluding or including specific records. Configure synchronization rules to ensure efficient and targeted data exchange between the two platforms.

6. Test and Validate Integration: Before fully deploying the integration, conduct thorough testing to validate its

functionality and performance. Test data synchronization processes, verify data accuracy and consistency, and confirm that integration settings are configured correctly. Address any issues or discrepancies identified during testing to ensure a smooth and reliable integration experience.

7. Monitor and Maintain Integration: Once integration is set up, monitor its performance and maintain it regularly to ensure continued functionality and reliability. Monitor data synchronization processes, address any errors or issues promptly, and stay informed about updates or changes that may impact integration compatibility or functionality. Regularly review integration settings and configurations to optimize performance and address evolving business needs.

Managing Leads And Opportunities Within Crm

Managing leads and opportunities within CRM (Customer Relationship Management) systems is crucial for maximizing sales effectiveness and driving business growth.

1. Capture Leads: Begin by capturing leads from various sources, including LinkedIn Sales Navigator, website inquiries, trade shows, and other marketing channels. Enter lead information into your CRM system, ensuring

that all relevant details are recorded accurately.

2. Qualify Leads: Qualify leads to determine their potential value and suitability as prospects. Use predefined criteria or lead scoring models to assess lead quality based on factors such as demographics, firmographics, behavior, and engagement level. Prioritize high-quality leads for further nurturing and engagement.

3. Assign Leads: Assign leads to sales representatives or teams based on predefined criteria such as territory, specialization, or workload. Ensure that leads are routed to the appropriate individuals or teams for follow-up and engagement, maximizing efficiency and responsiveness.

4. Nurture Leads: Implement lead nurturing strategies to engage and educate leads throughout the buyer's journey. Use personalized communication, targeted content, and timely follow-up to build relationships, address objections, and move leads closer to conversion. Track lead interactions and activities within your CRM system to gauge engagement and identify opportunities for further engagement.

5. Track Opportunities: As leads progress through the sales funnel, track opportunities within your CRM system to manage sales pipeline and forecast revenue. Create opportunity records to capture key details such as deal size, stage, expected close date, and probability of success. Regularly update opportunity records with relevant

information and status updates to ensure accuracy and visibility into sales performance.

6. Manage Activities: Schedule and manage activities related to lead and opportunity management, including calls, meetings, emails, and tasks. Use CRM features such as calendars, reminders, and activity tracking to stay organized and ensure timely follow-up and engagement. Document all interactions and communications within your CRM system to maintain a comprehensive record of customer interactions and engagement history.

7. Monitor Performance: Monitor lead and opportunity performance metrics to assess sales effectiveness and identify areas for improvement. Track key performance indicators (KPIs) such as lead conversion rate, opportunity win rate, average deal size, and sales cycle length to measure progress and identify trends. Use data insights to optimize sales processes, refine targeting strategies, and maximize revenue generation.

Streamlining Sales Processes With Automated Workflows

Automated workflows are a powerful tool for streamlining sales processes and improving efficiency within organizations. By automating repetitive tasks and standardizing processes, automated workflows enable sales teams to focus their time and energy on high-value activities such as building relationships, nurturing leads, and closing deals. Here's how automated workflows can streamline sales processes:

1. Lead Management: Automated workflows can streamline lead management processes by automatically assigning leads to sales representatives based on predefined criteria such as territory, industry, or lead score. When a new lead is captured, the workflow can trigger notifications and reminders to ensure timely follow-up and engagement.

2. Lead Nurturing: Automated workflows can facilitate lead nurturing by delivering personalized content and communications to leads at various stages of the buyer's journey. Workflows can be configured to send targeted emails, newsletters, or educational resources based on lead behavior, interests, or engagement level, helping to move leads through the sales funnel more effectively.

3. Opportunity Management: Automated workflows can streamline opportunity management processes by guiding sales representatives through predefined stages of the sales cycle. Workflows can automate tasks such as creating opportunity records, updating deal status, and sending notifications to stakeholders at key milestones, ensuring that opportunities are managed consistently and

efficiently.

4. Quote and Proposal Generation: Automated workflows can simplify the process of generating quotes and proposals by automating the creation, approval, and delivery of sales documents. Workflows can pull relevant information from CRM and pricing systems, generate customized quotes or proposals based on predefined templates, and route documents for approval and signature, reducing manual effort and accelerating the sales cycle.

5. Sales Forecasting and Reporting: Automated workflows can streamline sales forecasting and reporting processes by aggregating data from various sources, analyzing trends, and generating reports automatically. Workflows can pull data from CRM, ERP, and other systems, calculate key performance indicators (KPIs) such as pipeline value, win rate, and sales velocity, and generate dashboards or reports for sales managers and executives, providing real-time visibility into sales performance and trends.

6. Customer Onboarding and Retention: Automated workflows can improve customer onboarding and retention processes by delivering a seamless experience for new customers and proactively addressing their needs throughout the customer lifecycle. Workflows can automate tasks such as sending welcome emails, scheduling onboarding calls, and delivering training materials, ensuring that customers receive the support and

resources they need to succeed.

7. **Integration with Other Systems:** Automated workflows can integrate with other systems and tools used within the organization, such as marketing automation platforms, customer support systems, and finance systems, to facilitate seamless data exchange and collaboration across departments. Workflows can trigger actions and updates in other systems based on predefined triggers or conditions, ensuring data consistency and alignment across the organization.

By implementing automated workflows to streamline sales processes, organizations can improve efficiency, accelerate sales cycles, and drive revenue growth. With automation, sales teams can focus on what they do best—building relationships, closing deals, and delivering value to customers—while automated workflows handle the repetitive tasks and administrative overhead, enabling sales organizations to operate more effectively and competitively in today's fast-paced business environment.

# CHAPTER SEVEN

BEST PRACTICES AND STRATEGIES FOR SUCCESS

Building A Strong Network And Establishing Credibility

In the contemporary professional arena, cultivating and sustaining a robust network stands as a vital competency closely linked to one's overall professional merit. It acts as a pivotal determinant of success, portraying an individual's intrinsic value. Networking transcends mere exchange of business cards; it embodies an intricate craft requiring deliberate cultivation of meaningful relationships. It entails forging genuine connections that surpass surface-level interactions and establishing authentic rapport with individuals poised to contribute to professional advancement. Fostering a strong network demands investment of time and energy in nurturing these connections, comprehending the goals and aspirations of others, and extending support and aid whenever feasible.

Thriving in networking necessitates a proactive stance, entailing active engagement with peers, and pursuit of opportunities for collaboration, knowledge-sharing, and value provision. By actively participating in industry gatherings, affiliating with professional associations, and leveraging digital platforms, individuals can broaden their network and enhance their prospects of encountering invaluable connections.

According to Diane Helbig, a globally acknowledged consultant in business and leadership development, renowned author, acclaimed speaker, and proficient workshop facilitator, Networking is an investment in your business. It takes time (to spend on it) and when done correctly can yield great results for years to come." Building a strong network and establishing credibility are fundamental aspects of success in the modern business landscape. In today's interconnected world, relationships and reputation play a crucial role in career advancement, business growth, and professional success.

Networking strategies to fortify your professional connections

Establish Clear Objectives

Networking serves as a cornerstone for professional advancement, yet its efficacy hinges on defined objectives. Before immersing yourself in events or LinkedIn engagements, take a moment to introspect and discern your aims. Whether it's expanding your client base, exploring career opportunities, seeking mentorship, or gaining industry insights, crystallizing your goals magnifies the impact of networking pursuits. Pinpointing specific objectives, such as cultivating new business alliances, uncovering job leads, fostering mentor relationships, or acquiring industry intelligence, enables you to channel your efforts effectively and capitalize on networking prospects.

Embrace Authenticity

Authenticity lies at the heart of successful networking, fostering a favorable impression and engendering trust along your professional trajectory. Authenticity magnetizes individuals who resonate with your values and aspirations, rendering you relatable and inspiring mutual reciprocity. This authenticity catalyzes meaningful dialogues and invaluable revelations, which may burgeon into partnerships, collaborations, or friendships. In an era where trust is scarce, authenticity emerges as the linchpin of genuine networking triumph, as it holds sway as the most coveted asset in contemporary society.

Foster a Digital Footprint

In today's digital realm, nurturing an online presence is paramount for effective networking. Maintaining an updated LinkedIn profile complete with a professional image and succinct summary is indispensable. Actively sharing pertinent content and participating in substantive conversations amplifies your networking endeavors. Positioning yourself as a thought leader not only attracts fellow professionals but also nurtures profound connections. Social media platforms like LinkedIn, Twitter, and niche-specific forums serve as conduits to broaden your outreach. Your online persona should mirror your professional identity, harmonizing with your networking objectives and personal brand.

Engage in Networking Gatherings

Participation in both physical and virtual networking gatherings is invaluable for enlarging your professional circle. Whether it's conferences, workshops, webinars, or industry meet-ups, these events offer prime opportunities to connect with kindred spirits and industry luminaries. To extract maximum value from such occasions, crafting a succinct elevator pitch that eloquently introduces yourself is imperative. Additionally, ensuring you have a stash of business cards readily accessible at all times can leave a lasting impression and nurture meaningful connections within your domain.

Utilize Your Current Connections

To broaden your network and uncover fresh prospects, capitalize on your existing relationships and seek introductions from acquaintances, peers, and mentors who share your aspirations. Personal endorsements can serve as invaluable assets in networking, paving the way for more fruitful and meaningful connections. Endorsements from trustworthy sources bolster your credibility and foster trust with potential new contacts. Don't hesitate to leverage your current connections to expand your network and potentially open doors that might otherwise remain shut.

Engage in Volunteerism and Giving Back

Networking isn't solely about personal advancement; it's also about contributing to your community. Involvement in volunteer initiatives, offering your expertise, and providing assistance to others cultivate goodwill and increase the likelihood of receiving support in return. Professional networking underscores the importance of altruism, aligning with your skills and passions to make a positive difference in various causes and initiatives. Sharing insights and knowledge positions you as a reliable source, offering counsel, guidance, and mentorship. This spirit of generosity initiates a ripple effect of collaboration and support within your network.

Maintain Connections and Follow Through

Establishing and nurturing a network demands commitment and persistence. It entails following up with personalized messages, sustaining relationships through regular check-ins, sharing valuable insights, and arranging face-to-face meetings. Continuous communication forms the backbone of a robust network. In professional networking, it extends beyond initial introductions, with consistent follow-ups, information sharing, and personal interactions contributing to a vibrant and enduring network. Building strong connections and positioning oneself as a dependable source of support are vital for network success.

Practice Patience and Perseverance

Developing a substantial and influential professional network requires unwavering dedication and resilience. It's crucial to remain steadfast even in the face of delayed outcomes. Instead, persist in actively participating in relevant events, enhancing your digital presence, and nurturing meaningful relationships. Networking is a strategic endeavor that yields long-term benefits for your career, with its rewards gradually unfolding over time. Therefore, stay steadfast in your objectives, continue cultivating your network, and trust in the gradual growth that accompanies persistent effort.

Embrace Diversity in Connections

Fostering a thriving network necessitates embracing diversity in its broadest sense. Actively engaging with individuals from varied backgrounds, industries, and perspectives enriches your network with fresh insights, unique viewpoints, and untapped opportunities. By cultivating a diverse network, you not only enhance your professional growth but also contribute to creating a more inclusive and dynamic environment.

Embrace Lifelong Learning

In the realm of professional networking, knowledge holds immense value, making continuous learning imperative for success. Actively participating in workshops, delving into industry literature, and pursuing ongoing education are commendable habits. By staying abreast of the latest trends and advancements in your field, you not only bolster your expertise but also become a sought-after connection for others. Sharing up-to-date insights and engaging in informed conversations draws professionals closer, fortifying connections within your network and enhancing your networking prowess. As you continue to expand your knowledge and share valuable information, your network grows in power and influence.

By focusing on building genuine relationships, providing value, and demonstrating expertise, you can effectively build a strong network and establish credibility within your industry or field. Cultivate trust, reliability, and authenticity in your interactions, and strive to make meaningful contributions to your network that benefit both yourself and others. With dedication, consistency, and authenticity, you can build a strong network and establish credibility that will serve you well throughout your career.

Creating Compelling Inmail Messages And Outreach Templates

Crafting compelling InMail messages and outreach templates is essential for engaging prospects and driving meaningful conversations on LinkedIn Sales Navigator. Here's how you can create effective and impactful messages:

1. Personalization is Key: Personalize your messages to make them relevant and compelling to each recipient. Start by addressing the recipient by name and referencing specific details from their profile or recent activities.

Tailor your message to their interests, challenges, or goals to demonstrate that you've done your research and understand their needs.

2. Capture Attention with a Strong Subject Line: The subject line is the first thing recipients see, so make it attention-grabbing and compelling. Use clear and concise language that piques curiosity or offers value. Avoid generic or spammy subject lines, and instead, focus on providing a clear benefit or reason for the recipient to open your message.

3. Focus on Value and Benefits: In your message body, focus on the value and benefits that you can offer to the recipient. Clearly articulate how your product or service can solve their problems, address their pain points, or help them achieve their goals. Highlight specific benefits or outcomes that they can expect from engaging with you.

4. Keep it Concise and Scannable: Keep your message concise and easy to read by using short paragraphs, bullet points, and whitespace. Avoid long blocks of text that can overwhelm or discourage recipients from reading. Get to the point quickly and clearly communicate the key information or message that you want to convey.

5. Use Compelling Language and Tone: Use persuasive language and a friendly, conversational tone to engage recipients and encourage them to respond. Be professional yet personable, and avoid using jargon or overly formal

language that may alienate or confuse recipients. Focus on building rapport and establishing a connection with the recipient.

6. Include a Clear Call to Action (CTA): Every InMail message should include a clear call to action that prompts the recipient to take the next step. Whether it's scheduling a call, requesting more information, or downloading a resource, make it easy for recipients to respond by providing a clear and actionable CTA. Use compelling language that encourages immediate action and conveys a sense of urgency or importance.

7. Test and Iterate: Test different messaging strategies, subject lines, and CTAs to see what resonates best with your audience. Track metrics such as open rates, response rates, and conversion rates to gauge the effectiveness of your messages and identify areas for improvement. Iterate on your messaging based on feedback and results to continually optimize your outreach efforts.

Developing Consistent Engagement Strategies

Developing consistent engagement strategies is essential for building and nurturing relationships with your audience, whether it's prospects, customers, or industry peers. Consistency in engagement helps establish trust, credibility, and loyalty over time. Here's how you can develop effective and consistent engagement strategies:

1. Understand Your Audience: Start by understanding your audience's preferences, interests, and needs. Conduct research, gather data, and create buyer personas to better understand who your audience is and what they care about. Use this information to tailor your engagement strategies to resonate with your audience and address their specific pain points and interests.

2. Define Clear Objectives: Clearly define your engagement objectives and goals to guide your strategy. Whether it's increasing brand awareness, driving website traffic, generating leads, or fostering customer loyalty, having clear objectives will help you focus your efforts and measure success.

3. Choose the Right Channels: Identify the most effective channels for engaging with your audience based on their preferences and behavior. Whether it's social media, email, webinars, events, or other channels, choose the platforms where your audience is most active and receptive to your messages.

4. Create Valuable Content: Develop high-quality, relevant content that provides value to your audience. Whether it's blog posts, videos, podcasts, infographics, or whitepapers, create content that educates, entertains, or inspires your audience. Focus on solving their problems, answering their questions, or addressing their interests to keep them

engaged and coming back for more.

5. Be Consistent in Timing and Frequency: Consistency in timing and frequency is key to maintaining engagement with your audience. Develop a content calendar and schedule regular updates, posts, or communications to keep your audience informed and engaged. Whether it's daily, weekly, or monthly, stick to a consistent schedule to establish expectations and build anticipation.

6. Encourage Interaction and Participation: Actively encourage interaction and participation from your audience to foster engagement. Ask questions, solicit feedback, and invite discussions to spark conversation and dialogue. Respond promptly to comments, messages, and inquiries to show that you value and appreciate their engagement.

7. Measure and Analyze Results: Continuously monitor and analyze engagement metrics to evaluate the effectiveness of your strategies and tactics. Track metrics such as likes, shares, comments, clicks, opens, and conversions to gauge engagement levels and identify areas for improvement. Use data insights to refine your strategies, optimize your approach, and maximize engagement over time.

Measuring And Analyzing Performance Metrics

When considering social media analytics, platforms like Facebook and Instagram likely come to mind. However, LinkedIn should not be overlooked, especially in the B2B sector.

With over 1 billion members across 200 countries, LinkedIn boasts the highest user rate in the US, reaching over 214 million users.

Given its significant impact in B2B marketing, it's essential to explore how you can utilize LinkedIn analytics—a potent tool for monitoring, assessing, and enhancing your business's presence on this platform.

What Are Linkedin Analytics?

LinkedIn analytics refer to a set of metrics designed to evaluate the performance and impact of your posts, updates, and overall strategy on the platform. These statistical insights are instrumental in optimizing your LinkedIn marketing endeavors. LinkedIn analytics empowers you to uncover valuable insights regarding your audience demographics and their engagement with your company page and its content.

Why Monitor Linkedin Analytics?

Tracking LinkedIn analytics is essential for leveraging data to enhance your marketing strategy. Regularly assessing this data enables you to make informed decisions and optimize your investment effectively.

Here are the primary ways LinkedIn analytics can elevate your performance:

Understand audience engagement:

LinkedIn analytics provides insights into engagement metrics like likes, comments, and shares, offering valuable feedback on your social media interactions. By analyzing this data, you can identify content that resonates most with your target audience. This knowledge allows you to tailor your future posts to align with your audience's preferences and interests.

Assess competition:

Utilizing LinkedIn analytics enables you to conduct competitive analysis on social media. By comparing key metrics such as follower growth and content performance, you can identify strengths and areas for improvement relative to your competitors. This approach refines your social media strategy, positioning you for a competitive advantage in your industry.

Optimize ROI:

LinkedIn metrics such as lead generation, conversions, and campaign performance provide insights into the effectiveness of your social media efforts. By analyzing these metrics, you can pinpoint the most successful strategies and allocate resources accordingly. This data-driven approach enables you to optimize your marketing initiatives for maximum impact and business growth.

How To Access Linkedin Analytics

To access your LinkedIn business page analytics, follow these steps:

Step 1: Sign in to your LinkedIn account and navigate to your company page. Enter your LinkedIn admin view.

Step 2: On the left side of your screen, click on "Analytics."

Step 3: Within the Analytics tab, you'll find comprehensive insights categorized into Content, Visitors, Followers, Leads, Competitors, and Employee Advocacy. You can delve deeper to explore detailed metrics and trends.

Step 4: For a quick overview of the past 30 days, check the snapshot provided on the right side of your feed.

Note: Access to track analytics requires page admin privileges or "analyst" access.

The Essential Linkedin Metrics To Monitor

Navigating through extensive data can be overwhelming, but not every metric demands your immediate attention. Align your focus with your objectives to discern which metrics are pivotal and how they impact your business.

Outlined below are key LinkedIn analytics metrics that marketers should familiarize themselves with:

Visitor metrics:

LinkedIn visitor analytics offer insights into individuals exploring your company page on the platform. These visitors may not necessarily be followers or customers, but they've displayed a certain level of interest in your LinkedIn presence.

Page views: The overall count of times your page was accessed within a specified timeframe. This metric encompasses multiple views from the same user.

Unique visitors: The total count of distinct users who have visited your company page. It excludes repeat visits from the same user, providing an indication of unique interest in your profile.

Visitor demographics: This segment reveals the demographic details of those viewing your company page. It allows you to filter data based on location, industry, job role, company size, and seniority.

Make use of tools like Sprout Social to monitor both daily fluctuations and long-term averages effectively.

Follower metrics:

Followers signify individuals who actively subscribe to your company page and content, essentially forming your brand's community on LinkedIn.

Understanding the demographics and origin of your followers enables you to craft more engaging content and assess your brand's standing on the platform.

Total followers: The cumulative count of users following your company page, reflecting your brand's popularity and credibility, aligned with your goals and industry standards.

Organic followers: The number of followers acquired without investing in advertising. These followers discover your page through search engines, shares, or feeds, indicating genuine interest in your brand or content.

Sponsored followers: The count of followers obtained through advertising efforts. This metric allows you to evaluate the effectiveness of sponsored posts and campaigns.

Follower trends: Monitor the influx of new followers over a specified timeframe. Analyze whether your follower count is growing or declining and identify any abrupt changes in organic or sponsored followers through the follower metrics graph.

Follower demographics: Gain insights into the demographics of your followers, including location, seniority, industry, company size, and job function. Utilize this data to tailor content that resonates with your audience more effectively.

Sprout Social consolidates audience demographics data, offering a clear breakdown by seniority and job function, as illustrated below.

Engagement metrics:

Engagement metrics provide valuable insights into the performance of your LinkedIn posts and campaigns, offering insights into how your target audience interacts with your content.

Impressions: Reflects the number of times your post was displayed to LinkedIn users.

Average daily impressions per page: Indicates the average frequency with which users view any content associated with your page daily during the reporting period, excluding impressions on posts shared by others.

Video views: Indicates the number of times users watched your video content.

Reactions: Represents the number of users who reacted to your post, including Like, Celebrate, Support, Funny, Love, Insightful, and Curious. Receiving reactions indicates engagement with your content.

Comments: Signifies the total number of comments on your post, indicating active engagement and conversation initiation.

Post clicks: Reflects the number of times users clicked on links, media, the "more" icon, or your organization's page from your post within a specified timeframe.

Shares: Indicates the number of times your post was shared by LinkedIn users, contributing to increased reach, visibility, and brand awareness.

CTR (Click-Through Rate): Calculated as the percentage of clicks divided by impressions on a post, indicating how effectively your content prompts users to click on your company name, content, or logo.

Follows: Represents the total number of Follow clicks on your sponsored content.

LinkedIn engagement rate: Calculated using the formula (Clicks + Likes + Comments + Shares + Follows) / Impressions, expressed as a percentage, providing an overview of the average engagement level per post.

Total engagements: Indicates the total number of interactions users had with your post over its lifetime, encompassing likes, comments, shares, and clicks.

Sprout's dashboard offers tools to track and visualize engagement data for your LinkedIn page.

Creating Linkedin Analytic Report

To generate LinkedIn analytics reports within LinkedIn, you can export data or capture screenshots, depending on your account privileges. LinkedIn's native analytics offer various reports:

1. Campaign Performance/Ad Performance: Obtain crucial insights into your campaigns and ads. Download metrics such as spending, impressions, click-through rate, and engagement rate to evaluate their effectiveness.
2. Audience Network Campaign Performance/ Audience Network Ad Performance: Assess the performance of your campaigns and ads on LinkedIn and beyond. If you activate the LinkedIn Audience Network, compare statistics for LinkedIn, Audience Network, and overall performance.
3. Demographics: Gain deeper insights into your audience. Explore details like company names, job seniority, and functions of members engaging

with your campaigns and ads.
4. Conversion Performance/Conversion Ad Performance: Analyze the types of conversions your campaigns and ads are generating to gauge their actual impact.
5. Leads: Identify individuals interested in your product. Review responses to Lead Gen Forms associated with your campaigns to compile a list of engaged prospects.
6. Conversation Ad CTA Performance: Monitor button clicks for each action in your conversation ads to determine which prompts attract the most attention.
7. Placements Campaign Performance/Placements Ad Performance: Examine how your campaigns perform on LinkedIn and the Audience Network. Understand where you receive the highest engagement to optimize your planning and strategy.

Over 80% of B2B sales continue to take place on LinkedIn, underscoring the platform's significance for business success. With such a substantial portion of sales occurring here, it's crucial not to underestimate its importance. Enhancing your brand's reputation on LinkedIn requires dedicated effort, but the potential rewards are significant. Therefore, it's wise to consider investing in a reliable LinkedIn analytics tool. Doing so can yield substantial long-term benefits for your business.

CONCLUSION

In conclusion, LinkedIn Sales Navigator stands as a powerful tool in the modern sales professionals, it offers unparalleled access to insights, leads, and opportunities within the LinkedIn ecosystem. This book explores the evolution, features, and strategies for maximizing the potential of Sales Navigator to drive sales effectiveness and achieve business objectives.

From customizing preferences to leveraging third-party integrations, we have uncovered numerous ways to tailor Sales Navigator to fit individual workflows and amplify productivity. By staying updated on new features and adopting best practices, sales professionals can remain at the forefront of their field, equipped with the tools and knowledge needed to succeed in today's competitive landscape.

But beyond the technical aspects, the true power of Sales Navigator lies in its ability to foster meaningful connections and relationships with prospects and clients. By engaging authentically, providing value, and nurturing relationships over time, sales professionals can build trust, credibility, and loyalty, ultimately driving long-term success and growth.

As we conclude this journey through the world of LinkedIn Sales Navigator, I encourage you to embrace the insights and strategies shared in this book, and to continue exploring and innovating in your sales efforts. With Sales Navigator as your ally, the possibilities are limitless, and the potential for success is boundless.

Thank you for joining me on this exploration of LinkedIn Sales Navigator, and may your sales journey be filled with prosperity, fulfillment, and meaningful connections.

www.ingramcontent.com/pod-product-compliance
Lightning Source LLC
Chambersburg PA
CBHW070313230526
45470CB00002B/848